Seasons

Spring

Monica Hughes

Raintree

www.raintreepublishers.co.uk
Visit our website to find out more information about **Raintree** books.

To order:
☎ Phone 44 (0) 1865 888112
📄 Send a fax to 44 (0) 1865 314091
💻 Visit the Raintree Bookshop at **www.raintreepublishers.co.uk** to browse our catalogue and order online.

First published in Great Britain by Raintree, Halley Court, Jordan Hill, Oxford OX2 8EJ, part of Harcourt Education.
Raintree is a registered trademark of Harcourt Education Ltd.

... an Leake

... Liz Savery

Originated by Dot Gradations
Printed and bound in China by South China Printing Company

ISBN 978 1 844 21337 5 (hardback)
07 06 05 04
10 9 8 7 6 5 4 3 2

ISBN 978 1 844 21342 9 (paperback)
08
10 9 8 7 6

British Library Cataloguing in Publication Data
Hughes, Monica
Spring
508.2
A full catalogue record for this book is available from the British Library.

Acknowledgements
The publishers would like to thank the following for permission to reproduce photographs: Bruce Coleman Collection pp. **7, 14, 16, 18, 23b, 23d**; Bubbles pp. **11** (Ian West), **20** (Frans Rombout); Collections (Oliver Benn) p. **6**; FLPA/Foto Natura p. **23g**; Holt Studios International pp. **12, 23f** (Bob Gibbons); Mark Boulton p. **10**; NHPA pp. **9** (David Woodfall), **13** (E. A. Janes), **17** (Laurie Campbell); RSPCA p. **23e** (Stephen Oliver); Sally Greenhill p. **21**; Still Moving Pic. Co. (Ken Paterson) p. **8**; Trevor Clifford p. **5**; Tudor Photography p. **22**; Woodfall Wild Images pp. **4, 15, 19L, 23a**.

Cover photograph of a lamb, reproduced with permission of Oxford Scientific Films (Martyn Chillmaid).

Every effort has been made to contact copyright holders of any material reproduced in this book. Any omissions will be rectified in subsequent printings if notice is given to the publishers.

Contents

Some words are shown in bold, **like this**. You can find them in the glossary on page 23.

When is spring?

It is never clear when one season ends and the next one begins.

Spring is the season after winter and before summer.

We say that spring starts on 21 March.

March, April and May are the spring months.

What is the weather like in spring?

Spring is warmer than winter but cooler than summer.

The sun gets stronger as it gets higher in the sky.

The days are brighter and not so cold.

Sometimes there are lots of rain showers.

What clothes do we wear in spring?

We still wear warm clothes in spring.

They are lighter than clothes we wear in winter.

A raincoat and boots are
often useful.

What happens in towns in spring?

Spring sunshine often makes people want to clean their homes.

Spring is also a good time to think about beginning work in the garden.

What happens on farms in spring?

Spring is the start of the growing season.

Farmers **plough** the fields and plant seed.

Animals are put out to feed on the new grass.

What happens to animals in spring?

Many animals are born in spring.

Cows have calves and deer have **fawns**.

Hedgehogs and other animals have been sleeping all winter.

In spring they wake up from their **hibernation**.

What happens to birds in spring?

Spring is the time when birds build nests and lay eggs.

Then the parents are kept busy feeding the chicks.

Birds have to take care of their young.

What happens to plants in spring?

As the soil gets warmer, many plants begin to grow.

Trees are covered with new buds and **blossom**.

Woods are filled with bluebells and **daffodils** begin to bloom.

What celebrations take place in spring?

Easter is celebrated with different kinds of eggs.

Spring flowers are given as **posies** on Mother's Day.

People do maypole dancing to mark the end of spring and the beginning of summer.

Make a decorated egg

Ask an adult to boil an egg for half an hour in water mixed with food colouring.

When the egg is cool, polish it with cooking oil, paint it or decorate it with pieces of doily, sequins or ribbon.

Glossary

bloom
when a flower first opens up

blossom
flowers on trees in the spring

daffodil
a yellow flower that blooms in spring

fawn
young deer

hibernation
deep winter sleep

plough
use a machine to turn over soil to get it ready for planting

posies
small bunches of flowers

Index